MW00857238

BREAKTHROUGH
SPEAKING

Mark Sanborn,
CSP, CPAE

TREMENDOUS
LIFE BOOKS.COM

Breakthrough Speaking

Published by
Tremendous Life Books
118 West Allen Street
Mechanicsburg, PA 17055

717-766-9499   800-233-2665
Fax: 717-766-6565

www.TremendousLifeBooks.com

ISBN: 978-1-936534-34-4

Table of Contents

The Challenge

For leaders, the ability to communicate well and speak persuasively is a critical skill. All professional speakers, myself included, can continue to improve their skills. *Breakthrough Speaking* answers the questions I'm most frequently asked and shares some of the insights I've learned from 25 years of professional speaking.

According to Demosthenes, the ancient Greek known as the father of the speech, the most import principles of public speaking are "action, action, and action."

*Breakthrough speakers inspire
listeners to take action.*

Anyone with the courage to speak publicly can deliver a speech. The challenge is to deliver a speech that inspires your listeners to action. Public speaking that does not instigate action and change will ultimately be regarded as ineffective.

The Danish philosopher Søren Kierkegaard offers a parable of a speech that fails to meet the challenge. In the story *Tame Geese*, a gaggle of barnyard geese listened intently to a wild philosopher goose pontificate about the marvels of flight. He explained that they were born to fly, their wings were designed for it, and that flight was marvelous and liberating. The geese listened with rapt attention to the speech, but at its conclusion they waddled away to feed on the corn of their barnyard. Every time he spoke on the subject, they gathered attentively. Every time he concluded, they waddled back to what they were doing before.

I've related the story of the *Tame Geese* and asked both aspiring and accomplished speakers why the speech didn't work. Some respond that the geese must be lazy and indifferent. Others say that fear of flying or trying something new keeps the geese grounded. Or maybe habit is the culprit. The geese are used to waddling, and habits are hard to overcome—the problem was with the audience, in other words.

Some see a problem with the speech: the message wasn't personalized. The philosopher goose spoke only abstractly of flight so the geese couldn't see how it applied to them personally. And some say the problem is the speaker: the high goose himself doesn't fly. Since the geese watch what he does, as well as listen to what he says, they lack a role model for flight.

It's clear that the geese learn from the speech that they *can* fly—the geese understand intellectually that they are capable of flight—but they never put that understanding to the test. There is, after all, a tremendous leap between what one knows and what one does with that knowledge. And the speech never inspires the audience to translate its knowledge into action.

The parable of the pontificating goose and his inability to inspire his audience, the tame geese, to action epitomizes the challenge for anyone who wants to be a breakthrough speaker. *Breakthrough speakers inspire listeners to take action.*

Fortunately, the skills and techniques required for Breakthrough Speaking are learned, not inherited. There are steps you can take to become a speaker who inspires others to action, ranging from your speaking philosophy to your preparation to your performance. By working through the thoughtful approach outlined in this series, you can meet the challenge of *Breakthrough Speaking.*

Your Philosophy

According to Barna Research, only one of every four Americans has a worldview that guides their decisions and actions. It appears that most of us know *what* we do, for *whom* we do it, and *how much* we get paid to do it. The one thing we don't know is why we're doing it. To gauge the motivations of others, I often ask them, "What gets you out of bed in the morning?" Many of them offer a version of the same amusing but uninspiring response: "I have to go to the bathroom!" In other words, people are typically more motivated by their bladders than by their beliefs!

A first principle of Breakthrough Speaking is that it must originate in the speakers' beliefs, their own philosophy of speaking. The "whys" of speaking are every bit as important as the "whats" and the "how-tos." Why do you speak? Do you have a compelling purpose that drives each presentation you make? Before you can address the practice of speaking, you must have a philosophy of speaking. Before you approach the lectern or the microphone you must know why you are there.

The German philosopher Friedrich Nietzsche said, "He who has a reason *why* can bear almost any *how*" (emphasis added).

To be effective, to motivate others to act, and to achieve breakthrough results in their lives, a speaker must have a compelling motivation behind his or her own actions.

My own philosophy of speaking, for example, is based on the following three premises:

1. The everyday experience of life for an individual or organization is one

of pain, problems, or discomfort. I don't mean this in a melodramatic way. Think of pain and discomfort —personally and organization-ally—that comes from responding to challenges like unhappy customers or unpleasant employees; competition that threatens to take customers and market share; and setbacks like regulatory changes or even crises.

2. Despite the presence of pain in life, everyday experience offers the opportunity for unlimited joy. That is, joy is always possible. We can reframe what happens and respond in such a way that we triumph rather than suffer; we enjoy rather than endure.

3. My opportunity as a professional speaker is to help audiences with the tasks of understanding the pain of life, dealing with that pain, and/or experiencing life's joy. I am most successful when I

can help an audience accomplish all three tasks.

What is your philosophy of speaking? Why do you aspire to speak and what do you hope to accomplish?

To begin developing your speaking philosophy, consider the expectations of an audience. Almost any audience will have two principal expectations of you. First, your listeners expect you to make them feel good (or better) about themselves and their situation. Second, they expect you to give them some insight, tools, and direction that will help them live or do business more successfully. My three-point philosophy of speaking addresses both of these audience expectations—and your philosophy should, too.

If you really want to inspire others to action through speaking, you must first be inspired to speak by your own belief in what you are doing—your philosophy of speaking. A philosophy of speaking that motivates you to action is the first step toward Breakthrough Speaking.

The Psychology & Practice of Persuasion

Aristotle defined rhetoric as "the art of persuasion." He identified the three main elements of persuasion: *character, emotion, and logic*. His wisdom still holds true today.

An audience's judgment of a speaker's **character** will determine whether they accept the messenger and therefore the message. What does it take to make an audience comfortable enough to trust you and believe in the validity of your message, in your "character?" In short, credibility and rapport.

Credibility comes from the audience's belief that you are qualified to address your subject, whether through expertise or experience. For example, my credibility on the subject of speaking comes from the fact that I've given over 2,200 paid presentations over a span of 25 years. Your introduction can establish your credibility or you may subtly allude to your credentials in a way that does not seem boastful or arrogant.

Rapport is based on a connection, a feeling that you and your audience are on the same "wavelength," that you have something in common. We tend to accept and like people we believe are like us. So it's important to establish common ground with your audience. And the one thing you can always have in common with your audience is *their best interest*. You can quickly establish rapport with an audience when they feel that you are interested in providing something of value to them, that the message is more important than the messenger. Communicate sincerely to your audience that you are there to be of service to them. If they sense that you are there to meet your own needs, rather than theirs, it will be difficult, if not impossible, for you to establish rapport with them.

The next component of persuasion is *emotion*. Most decisions are based, at least in part, on emotion. Once we make an emotional decision, we then sort out the logical reasons that support it. To be a breakthrough speaker, you must connect with people emotionally. Don't confuse emotional connection with maudlin manipulation. Effective ways to evoke emotion in an audience include stories, parables, metaphors, and examples that demonstrate the human element and emotion of your message. You can also use amplification, that is, to amplify the "pain" of the problems that you address and then magnify the "relief" of the solutions you provide.

People are capable of experiencing a wide range of emotions. What emotions do you try to evoke through your speaking? Since listeners want to feel good about what you have to say, design your message in a way that results in positive emotions.

Finally, you must use *logic* to persuade. If your message is not logical, then your credibility, rapport, and emotional appeal will be lost. When listeners feel good about what they are hearing, they will consciously or unconsciously check to see that the message is also logical, that it makes sense, and rings true. Logic validates emotion.

Cicero, the great Roman orator, insisted that speakers must know their subjects inside and out. You should be able to support your argument with facts, data, or anecdotes that prove your point. Accuracy is important, too. If you misquote a source or use statistics incorrectly, some listeners will catch your mistake and wonder about the validity of your entire speech. In short, know your stuff and use the stuff you know to make your point *logically*.

To keep your message on a persuasive track, just remember that listeners are always asking these three questions on a subconscious level:

1. Why should I listen to this speaker? *Character (Credibility and Rapport)*

2. Why do I care? *Emotion*

3. Why should I believe or do what this speaker says? *Logic*

How to Design a Breakthrough Speech

The real hard work that goes into a presentation should take place before you step up to the podium. Effective presentations are *designed* before they are delivered. If you aspire to be a breakthrough speaker, design your speech with the following components in mind.

Outcomes. When designing your speech, begin at the end. In other words, first determine your desired outcomes. What do you want your listeners to think, feel, and do as the result of your presentation? Design your speech around the thoughts, feelings, and actions you want to inspire in the audience. Think of the main point or message you want your audience to take away. Make sure all the elements of your speech point toward that message.

In his book *Flow: The Psychology of Optimal Experience*, Mihaly Csikszentmihalyi describes the effect of an excellent painting on an attentive observer: "What this person sees in a painting is not just a picture, but a 'thought machine' that includes the painter's emotions, hopes, and ideas—as well as the spirit of the culture and the historical period in which he lived." In the same way, think of your presentation as a "thought machine" that you are painting with words, tone, pacing, and gestures. Use the entire canvas of your speech, your "thought machine" to bring your audience to the desired outcome.

Title. Surprisingly, something as simple as a title can make a big difference in the appeal of your presentation. The title should

BREAKTHROUGH SPEAKING

both grab listener attention and promise a benefit. For example, a high school in Virginia had trouble filling a course titled *Home Economics for Boys*. The title obviously wasn't grabbing the audience's attention. When the school administrators renamed the course *Bachelor Living*, 120 boys immediately signed up.

Your Message. Of course, it isn't enough to present just any old message. You must present *your* message. Goethe said, "In this world there are so few voices, and so many echoes."

Consider what it is about your topic that matters to you, that affects you the most and that makes it *yours*. Your speech should not just be a dry report of facts and information. Rather, it should bring your unique perspective to the audience. When you discover your message, your passion for your subject will come across. Your passion is what will make your speech memorable To bring your message into focus, think about how you would want an audience member to answer the question, "What was that speech about?"

Illustrations. Stories, examples, parables, metaphors. When I was younger, I read several books by Norman Vincent Peale. I always wondered why he told such long stories to make a relatively brief point. It wasn't until I was older that I realized people don't remember the points you make—they remember the stories you tell. And it's by remembering your stories that they recall the points you made. Stories are like mental coat hooks: they are places for listeners to hang ideas.

Where do you get the best stories to illustrate your ideas? From your own life experiences! Think back; review your life. Look for the important lessons you've learned, then recall the experiences, sad as well as happy, that taught you those lessons.

Just as variety is said to be the spice of life, so it is with illustrations in your speech. Be aware of the many illustrations in the world around you. They're everywhere and in everything—from nursery rhymes to *The Wall Street Journal*—and they're available to anyone who keeps an eye out for them. The people in your life are a gold mine of illustrations. Some of my best material has come from cab drivers, airline attendants, my clients, and even my postal carrier. The world is filled with ordinary people doing and saying extraordinary things. Be an observer of people, and share what you've learned from interacting with them.

Humor. George Burns once said, "I am a comedian. If people do not laugh, I'm a humorist. If people don't get it at all, I'm a singer. If I sing and they laugh, I'm a comedian." The best use of humor in a speech is to illustrate a point. If your audience thinks your point of humor is side-splitting, that's great. But even if they don't think it's funny, it will still help get your message across and help establish rapport.

Entertainment. Finally, keep in mind that education and information are typically best delivered on the wings of entertainment. In fact, probably the best advice on speaking I ever received was 20 years ago from then Ohio legislator David Johnson who told me that every audience wants to be entertained. Today's successful speaker is an informer, but also a performer. It is vital for a breakthrough speaker to capture and hold an audience's attention, and to do so, you must be interesting at the least and, ideally, entertaining.

The Trade Secret for a Breakthrough Performance

The old British army adage, "Proper Preparation Prevents Poor Performance," referred to military maneuvers but it applies just as well to speaking. Lack of preparation is the number-one reason that speakers fail. On the other hand, good preparation can often compensate for a lack of natural talent. Knowing all aspects of your presentation inside and out will help you deal with anxiety and distractions.

First, you must know your material. Do your homework. Study and master your subject matter. Know your speech backwards and forwards. Make sure your information is accurate and up-to-date. When you are completely comfortable with your subject, your confidence will be projected to the audience.

Next, do some homework for extra credit. Who is your audience and how does your message apply to them? No one likes to sit through generic, one-speech-fits-all presentations. People want to hear information that has been personalized to their situation. Are you speaking to doctors or lawyers? How does your message apply to their professions? Speaking to accountants and brokers? How does your message affect the financial industry? Speaking to sales and marketing professionals? How can your message help them reach their goals? Even a little bit of prior research can help you tailor your message to your audience.

You can even try getting a little insider information on your specific audience. Get the names of several people who will be in your audience. Contact those people and ask for a few minutes of their time. Conduct pre-program interviews with them to learn how best to tailor your presentation. Understanding your audience and their unique challenges, worries, fears, and desires will prepare you to establish a rapport with them and strike their emotional chords.

You should also make sure you understand the venue and its parameters and limitations. Large room or small? Microphone or not? Projectors? Internet connections? In other words, avoid last minute logistical surprises that will throw you off course and prevent you from delivering a breakthrough performance.

Finally, rehearse your speech. And rehearse it again. Practice may not make you perfect, but it will make you better. And enough practice can make you great. You should rehearse your speech until you are completely comfortable delivering it from start to finish.

You may not be able to control who your audience is, their willingness to listen, or their receptivity to your message. But you are in complete control of how prepared you are when you speak to them. Preparation and practice are the most important elements of any presentation. If, at minimum, proper preparation prevents poor performance, then great preparation will produce breakthrough performances.

The Breakthrough Performance

You've designed and prepared your speech. You believe in your message and are rooted in your philosophy of speaking. Now it's showtime, where philosophy and preparation meet performance. Here are eight pointers for making it a breakthrough performance.

First, don't overlook the importance of your introduction. It accomplishes two vital tasks—it establishes your credibility, giving your audience a reason to listen to you, and it sets the tone for your presentation. Don't think of the introduction simply as fluff-stuff that happens before you speak. It is a part of your presentation. So work with the person who will be introducing you. Provide him or her the most appropriate information about yourself in a form that offers maximum benefit. Most professional speakers use a prepared introduction. You should too.

Second, remember that anxiety is OK. In his book *Emotional Intelligence*, Daniel Goleman addresses the subject of anticipatory anxiety. He says that skilled people use anxiety to motivate themselves to prepare adequately and perform well. I still get nervous before speaking, even after speaking to 2,000-plus audiences over the years. If I didn't, there would be something wrong with me.

Anxiety generates adrenaline—it makes you alert and keeps you at your best. If you experience no anxiety, you are either over-confident or asleep—and neither state leads to breakthrough speaking. The trick is to use anxiety to fuel your performance rather than let it become an obstacle.

Third, let your humanity show through. My colleague Winnie Shows describes what she calls "The Goldfinger Effect" in the art of speaking. Years ago, the movie *Goldfinger* prompted a question about a character painted completely in gold. What would happen if someone were covered in gold paint? Would one's cells suffocate? Could it cause death? The general agreement, according to Winnie, was that one could paint the body gold if a little space was left unpainted. Likewise, she points out that a highly polished presentation is good, but it is critically important that the speaker's humanity shows through.

I agree wholeheartedly with Winnie's illustration. If your presentation is too polished, people will think you're too perfect, and that can reduce your rapport with them. So leave a little of your presentation unpolished, perhaps a few segments where you add a personal aside. Apply "The Goldfinger Effect" and your listeners will know that you are human, like they are, and they will be more receptive to your message.

Fourth, make the most of your opening. Memorize the first part of your presentation and practice it so that it seems natural rather than stiff or "canned." Knowing exactly how you're going to begin and being intimately familiar with your opening will prevent anxiety-caused forgetfulness.

Also, remember that your opening is your best chance to break your audience's preoccupation with circumstances and concerns outside the presentation room. People may be sitting quietly in front of you and looking at you, but that doesn't mean that they are paying attention to you. You must open in a way that will break through their preoccupation and capture their imagination. Your audience needs immediate proof that the rest of your message is worth sticking around for. An interesting illustration, a surprising quote, or a challenging question are just three ways to open your message with attention-grabbing power.

Fifth, don't read your speech. If you feel tempted to do so, remember that it would be more effective to give your listeners their own copies and let them read your presentation for themselves. Breakthrough speakers don't read their speeches, they deliver them.

Sixth, use variety. Nobody enjoys a monotone presentation. Good conversation is lively and animated. So, too, is effective public speaking. Talk softly. Talk loudly. Vary your tone, energy, pace, and emotion. Think of breakthrough speaking as a musical score, and make full use of the range of notes available to you.

Much has been written about the importance of passion in speaking. I would offer two cautions about this subject. First, remember that passion without technique is misdirected. While listeners may admire your passion, they won't be positively impacted until you learn how to use it to bolster your delivery. Second, passion is not about rabid enthusiasm or the decibel level of your voice. It is about the conviction of your words.

Seventh, make it easy for your listeners to act. Give them very specific suggestions about what you want them to do as a result of your presentation. Breakthrough speaking is designed to spur audience members to action. So make sure they know what appropriate actions to take and how to take them.

Eighth and finally, have a strong closing. When you finish, finish. Avoid false closings at all costs. A false closing suggests to the audience that you are going to end, but then you continue to cover additional points or material. In such a situation, listeners feel tricked, and your effectiveness is seriously compromised.

Know exactly how you are going to conclude (just as you knew exactly how you were going to begin). Your closing is the last point people will remember, so make it memorable.

After the Applause, Analyze the Impact

Your speech may be over, but the work of Breakthrough Speaking is not. As your audience files out of the room, you should begin to review and analyze your performance. Did your presentation have the impact you sought? Did you inspire the members of your audience to see things in a different light and to change? By conducting a "post-mortem" examination of every performance, you can get a true sense of what works and what doesn't, and you can make your presentation even better for the next time.

You can begin your post-performance analysis immediately by making some quick, brief notes to yourself right after the speech. During a speech, you will get a sense of the highlights and lowlights of the audience response and your own effectiveness in communicating your message. You should jot down your thoughts about these moments as quickly as possible because you are likely to forget them once you have left the stage and your selective memory takes over.

Also, immediately following your speech, some members of the audience may approach you with some feedback. People who come up to you afterwards will be, for the most part, positive. That's because people typically hesitate to confront a speaker face-to-face if they didn't enjoy him or her. Expect that the audience members you talk to afterwards will be kind, if not completely honest.

You need to solicit broader constructive feedback from your audience. Good friends and relatives (who view your performance) can be a source of honest feedback, but only if they love you enough to tell you the truth. Ask them for their opinion of your presentation in these three areas: what worked, what didn't work, and how you can improve. You might also follow up with the event organizers and even audience members. Try sending them a brief thank you that invites them to say what they liked and what they didn't about your performance.

In the days following your performance, review your presentation, considering your notes and feedback. If your presentation was recorded, review the audio or video of it and critique yourself and your impact on the audience. In this light, consider how your presentation could be improved for even greater impact. A little change of emphasis here or there can make all the difference.

Also, remember that you can't affect an entire audience. I used to be disappointed if an audience didn't laugh, applaud, or get excited at the points I thought the audience should. But then I made an important discovery: breakthrough speaking isn't about affecting an audience. It's about affecting individuals in that audience. When they leave the presentation room, they are no longer an audience, and, ultimately, any change will be at an individual level. When someone comes to me at the end of a presentation and says, "I just want you to know that what you said today made a difference to me," I am gratified. I know I've achieved success where it counts—at the individual level.

It is important that you know the difference between a *good audience* and *good work*. I have made really good presentations to which my audience didn't overtly respond, and I have made less-than-spectacular presentations that my audience greeted with cheers and applause. If you evaluate your speaking on the basis of audience response, you might be misled. Instead, ask yourself, "Did I do good work today?"

What qualifies as good work? When I have designed a presentation that will deliver value for listeners, when I have then prepared, practiced, and presented it to the best of my ability—that's when I have done good work.

Why Bother?
Speaking About What Matters and Making it Matter

Once I was on the 50-yard line of Atlanta's Georgia Dome. No, I wasn't playing quarterback for the Atlanta Falcons. I had just finished speaking to a group of 100 who had gathered for a departmental meeting.

Afterwards, as I was talking with a few audience members, a man who had been standing near the field entrance approached me. He extended his hand and said, "I'm one of the bus drivers. We weren't invited to attend your presentation, but I stood in the back anyway. I like hearing speakers and learning new ideas, and I want you to know that you really encouraged me. You see, I'm an inventor. I've invented a new seat cushion that people can use at stadiums like this one. I agreed with practically everything you said, and your words have encouraged me to keep trying."

Although my client was happy with my presentation that day, my biggest reward was not the fee I received. It was the feedback of an appreciative individual who wasn't even supposed to be there! Without even knowing it, I had achieved a breakthrough.

If your presentations are rooted in your philosophy of speaking, if you are motivated to deliver a message you believe in, and if you devote the time and effort to preparation that your message deserves, chances are very good you will break through with someone.

Public speaking is the oldest form of mass communication. It was part of the formation of democracy in ancient Greece and Rome and the most important part of their school curriculums. Presenting a message to a live audience of listeners offers an immediacy that no other medium can provide. Think of the difference between live theater and watching a movie on TV. Even in the age of social media, no other form of communication has as much power to inspire and to change as the breakthrough speech. In fact, speeches delivered in the public square were the original social network!

If you have a message to deliver—one that you sincerely believe in—and your philosophy moves you to want to inspire and change people, the best way to reach them is by mastering Breakthrough Speaking. If your heart and your effort are in your speaking, your message will break through with some, if not all, of your audience almost every time. And when members of your audience approach you after a speech to say something like, "What you said really encouraged me," you have a real sense of "mission accomplished."

So remember—you never know who's watching and listening. In a sense, our lives are speeches given to many various audiences. These speeches can impact others we may never know in ways we may never understand. Often, it's the reward of an unexpected and heartfelt "thank you" that becomes the most valued of all.

And that's when you know you've achieved a breakthrough.

More Information About the Author

Mark Sanborn, CSP, CPAE is president of Sanborn & Associates, Inc., an idea studio for leadership development. He is an award-winning speaker and the author of the best-selling books, *The Fred Factor: How Passion In Your Work and Life Can Turn the Ordinary Into the Extraordinary,* and *You Don't Need a Title to be a Leader: How Anyone Anywhere Can Make a Positive Difference. His latest books are Up, Down or Sideways: How to Succeed when Times are Good, Bad or*

In Between and Fred 2.0: New Ideas on How to Keep Delivering Extraordinary Results.

To obtain additional information for growing yourself, your people, and your business (including free articles), visit www. MarkSanborn.com.

For information about having Mark speak for your group, call (303) 683-0714.

BREAKTHROUGH SPEAKING NOTES

_____

_____

_____

_____

_____

_____

_____

_____

_____

_____

_____

_____

_____

_____

_____

_____

_____

_____

_____

_____

_____

_____

_____

_____

_____

_____

_____

_____

_____

_____

_____

_____

_____

_____

_____

_____

_____

_____

_____

_____

_____

_____